Instant Pot Cookbook

─ ─ ─ ─ ─ ❧❧❧❧ ─ ─ ─ ─ ─

5 Ingredients or Less – Quick, Easy and Healthy Meals for Your Family

D1056478

Tyler Smith

Table of Contents

Introduction

Thank you for getting your personal copy of, *"Instant Pot Cookbook: 5 Ingredients or Less – Quick, Easy and Healthy Meals for Your Family."*

The Instant Pot is one of the best versatile kitchen appliances to use for a wide range of recipes. It can braise, boil, pressure cook, sauté, shallow-fry, slow cook, and steam dishes all in one pot. It can cook everything from simple porridges, to quick savory snacks, and even desserts.

The following chapters will provide you with over 100 recipes that you can prepare using your Instant Pot. This book features easy to follow steps and strategies on how to use the Instant Pot to come up with a variety of great recipes. It contains recipes that are healthy, quick and easy to follow.

It's not necessary for you to deprive yourself in order to eat clean and healthy. All you have to do is choose the right ingredients and eat moderately. Use the recipes in this book to guide you in planning your healthier and more nutrient rich meals.

Lastly, this book contains information on how to use the **Instant Pot** properly, in case this is your first time using this machine, or you would like to know a few tricks to amplify the use of this cooker.

Thanks again for getting a copy of this book. I hope you enjoy it.

Instant Pot Pressure Cooker Basics

The **Instant Pot** is a multi-function, countertop 11 psi electric cooker. It can be used as a rice cooker, slow cooker, steamer, warmer, and pressure cooker. Newer models like IP-DUO and IP-SMART have: browning, pasteurization,  sautéing, and yogurt making functions.

Instant Pot machines come in three sizes: five, six, and eight quarts. Machines with large capacities are best for making homemade steamed bread and yogurt.

These can be used for pasteurizing milk and for making cheeses. These are also suitable for making large meals for parties, or if you want to freeze large volumes of dishes (e.g. broths, soups, stews, etc.) for later consumption.

Each **Instant Pot** comes with a crockpot (stainless steel inner pot/sleeve,) a removable lid with steaming vent, steaming basket, and a removable trivet.

Benefits of using Instant Pot

1. This is the quintessential set-it-and-walk-away all-in cooker. All you need to do is to:

   - Prepare the ingredients beforehand. Place these into the crockpot.

   - Twist and lock the lid. Seal or unseal steamer valve (depending on function.)

- Set desired function (e.g. PRESSURE COOK, STEAM, etc.). Set the timer.

- Walk away and return after the prescribed cooking time. (See **Note**.)

- Release the pressure. Remove the lid.

- Stir in remaining ingredients, if any.

- Ladle dish into serving containers. Garnish as needed. Serve. Eat.

Note: **Instant Pot** has a "KEEP WARM" (warming) function, which automatically activates after the timer goes off. Unless it is specified in the recipe(s) that you need to turn off the machine *immediately after cooking,* there is no need to rush back to the cooker. You can return to the kitchen whenever you want.

Pressure cooking means that you can cook meals 75% to 100% faster than boiling/braising on the stovetop, and baking/roasting in a conventional oven.

This is especially helpful for vegan meals that entail the use of dried beans, legumes, pulses, etc. Instead of pre-soaking these ingredients for hours prior to use, you can pour these directly into the crockpot, add water, and pressure cook these for several minutes. (See **Appendix I** for recommendations.)

2. Use **Instant Pot** to make meals in advance. The machine automatically activates the KEEP WARM function after each cooking cycle. This allows you to prepare meals in the morning, so that you can come home to a warm dinner. Or, set up the **Instant Pot** before going to bed so that breakfast is cooked when you wake up.

How to use the Instant Pot

The **Instant Pot** has automatic: BEAN/CHILI, MEAT/STEW, MULTIGRAIN, PORRIDGE, POULTRY, PRESSURE, RICE, SAUTE, SLOW COOK, SOUP, STEAM, WARM, and YOGURT functions.

For this book, we will concentrate on how to use the PRESSURE or pressure cooker function.

The two easiest ways to do so is to:

<u>Step 1</u>:

1. Pour all the ingredients into the crockpot.

2. Close lid. Twist it to lock. Beeping sounds will indicate if machine is sealed.

3. Seal valve (steaming vent) on top of the lid by turning the knob towards the SEALING option (the opposite of which is VENTING.) By doing so, the machine automatically assumes that you are opting for NATURAL PRESSURE RELEASE. This means that the lid remains sealed until the pressure within the crockpot dissipates or lessens, extending the cooking time by up to 20 minutes.

4. Press the PRESSURE (pressure cooker) button.

5. Wait for 10 seconds without doing anything. The machine will automatically go to its preset option, which is at: HIGH PRESSURE at 30 minutes.

6. After the cooking cycle, and the NATURAL PRESSURE RELEASE, the machine will automatically activate the KEEP WARM function.

7. This is the only time you can safely open the lid.

Step 2:

1. Pour all the ingredients into the crockpot.

2. Close lid. Twist it to lock. Seal valve.

3. Set machine on MANUAL mode. This still means that you are still pressure cooking, but you can change settings.

4. Choose either LOW PRESSURE or HIGH PRESSURE button. Most of the time though, dishes need to be cooked on high pressure.

5. Set the timer by pushing the plus [+] or minus [-] buttons right above the PRESSURE button, to increase or decrease cooking time, respectively.

6. Wait for 10 seconds without doing anything. The machine will then start cooking according to your "instructions."

7. If the recipe calls for turning off the machine immediately after cooking, press the KEEP WARM button twice to CANCEL after the cooking cycle. Or, you can simply unplug the machine.

8. If the recipe recommends QUICK PRESSURE RELEASE, carefully turn the knob on the lid towards

VENTING. Keep your face and hands away from the steam as it comes out to prevent second-degree burns. Depending on how much moisture is inside the crockpot, venting can take between fifteen seconds to five minutes.

9. Only when the steam has subsided can you safely open the lid.

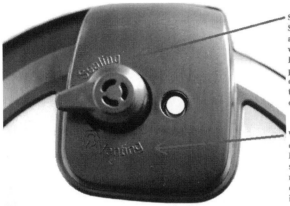

Sealing = valve is closed. Steam cannot escape, which allows pressure to build up within. NATURAL PRESSURE RELEASE means waiting for pressure to subside on its own for 15 to 20 minutes. In the meantime, the pressure cooker remains sealed.

Venting = valve is manually opened. This is called QUICK PRESSURE RELEASE. After steam is released (1 to 2 minutes,) the pressure cooker can be opened immediately.

There are some recipes that require additional steps (e.g. browning, liquid reduction, etc.), so it is best to follow the recommended procedure when cooking.

Important: Instant Pot should have at least one cup of liquid during cooking to prevent contents from sticking to the bottom of the crockpot.

If recipes for pressure cooking require large volumes of liquid, pour in just enough to fill 2/3 of the crockpot. This is to ensure that there is space for pressure and steam to build up within.

For other cooking functions, never fill the pot over the MAX line indicator to avoid spillage.

If you made a mistake with the settings, or you simply want to add a few more ingredients to the crockpot, double press the KEEP WARM button to CANCEL. Opt for a QUICK PRESSURE RELEASE and wait for the steam to subside, if any. Reset the machine as needed.

For other functions and more details: check product manual.

Breakfast

01 Scotch Eggs

Prep Time: 5 minutes; **Cook Time**: 18 minutes

Recommended Serving Size: 1 egg; **Serves**: 4

Ingredients:

- 4 large eggs

- 1 tbsp. vegetable oil

- 1 pound ground country sausage

Directions:

1. Cook the eggs first. Begin by putting the steamer basket in your instant pot. Pour a cup of water into your pot, and then sit the eggs in. Place your pot on high pressure for six minutes. Once done, use the natural release for six minutes. Do a quick pressure release to release the remaining pressure. Place the eggs in cold water to cool.

2. Once chilled, peel the eggs. Press a quarter of a pound of sausage around each egg. You are essentially making a sausage meatball around the egg. Turn the instant pot to sauté and add the oil. Brown the Scotch eggs on all sides. Turn them as needed. Once brown, remove from instant pot and place to the side.

3. The rack should be added to the pot and a cup of water poured in. Place the scotch eggs on the rack and cook for six minutes on high pressure. When finished use quick release for the pressure and enjoy.

02 Fruit Yogurt

Prep Time: 5 minutes; **Cook Time**: 12 hours, 5 minutes

Recommended Serving Size: 1 jar; **Serves**: 4

Ingredients:

- 4 pint jars
- 4 tbsp. milk powder
- 5 1/3 cup milk
- 2 cups chopped fruit
- 4 tbsp. sugar

Directions:

1. Pour 1 ½ cups water into the instant pot, and set the grate in.

2. Add 1 1/3 cups milk to each of your jars and loosely screw on the lids. Sit the jars in the pot. Set on yogurt for two minutes. Once pressure releases naturally, remove the lid and allow the jars to cool, and carefully remove.

3. Add the yogurt culture, 1 tablespoon milk powder, and 1 tablespoon sugar to each jar. Stir together well. Mix in a ½ cup of fruit to each jar. Stir. Loosely place on the lids. Set to yogurt setting for 12 hours.

4. Refrigerate leftovers.

03 Egg Muffin

Prep Time: 10 minutes; **Cook Time**: 20 minutes

Recommended Serving Size: 1 muffin; **Serves**: 4

Ingredients:

- Shredded cheese
- 4 large eggs
- 1 onion, diced
- 4 slices bacon, crumbled
- ½ tsp lemon pepper seasoning

Directions:

1. Pour 1 ½ cups of water into your pot. Set the steamer basket inside the pot.

2. Beat the eggs together with the seasonings. Equally separate the cheese, onion, and bacon between four silicon cups. Separate the beaten eggs among the silicon cups. Sit cups into the instant pot.

3. Cover with the lid and seal into place. Set the pot high for eight minutes. Let the pressure release for a couple of minutes before using the quick pressure release.

04 Chunky Applesauce

Prep Time: 10 minutes; **Cook Time**: 15 minutes

Recommended Serving Size: 1 cup; **Serves**: 8

Ingredients:

- 1 tsp. cinnamon
- 10 large apples
- ¼ cup water
- ¼ cup sugar

Directions:

1. Take the apples and peel and core them. Slice them into even slices. Set the apples in the instant pot. Add everything else in and mix it all together. Set the pot to high and cook for four minutes. Once finished, use quick release for the pressure.

2. Using a spoon, break up the large pieces of apples until you have the chunkiness you want. You can also use an immersion blender if you want a smoother texture.

05 Breakfast Quinoa

Prep Time: 5 minutes; **Cook Time**: 1 hour

Recommended Serving Size: ½ cup; **Serves**: 6

Ingredients:

- ½ tsp vanilla
- 2 ¼ cups water
- 2 tbsp. maple syrup
- ¼ tsp. ground cinnamon
- 1 ½ cup quinoa

Directions:

1. Rinse off the quinoa. Place all of the above ingredients in the instant pot. Mix them together well.

2. Turn the pot to high and cook for one minute. Allow the mixture to sit for ten minutes once done. If there is any pressure left, use the quick release function to get rid of it. Use a fork to fluff the quinoa.

3. Serve with a splash of milk or desired toppings.

06 Egg Casserole

Prep Time: 5 minutes; **Cook Time**: 37 minutes

Recommended Serving Size: ½ cup; **Serves**: 4

Ingredients:

- Favorite breakfast meat, cooked
- 7 eggs
- 2 tbsp. milk
- Cheese of choice

Directions:

1. Grab a bowl and break the eggs into it. Pour in the milk and then add the meat. Whisk them all together. Season with some pepper and salt.
2. When well mixed, place the trivet in the instant pot, and add a cup of water.
3. Spray a four-cup oven safe dish with cooking spray.
4. Give the eggs another stir and the pour them into the baking dish.
5. Place the dish in the instant pot.
6. Close the lid and seal into place. Cook the food on high for 17 minutes.
7. Allow the pressure to release naturally. Take the dish out, carefully, it will be hot.
8. Let it sit a couple of minutes. Sprinkle with some cheese and enjoy.

07 Chinese Steamed Eggs

Prep Time: 5 minutes; **Cook Time**: 15 minutes

Recommended Serving Size: ½ cup; **Serves**: 2

Ingredients:

- ½ tbsp. fish sauce
- 2 extra large eggs
- 1 cup chicken stock
- 1 tbsp. water
- ½ tbsp. soy sauce

Directions:

1. Grab a bowl and break the eggs into it. Mix well. Add the chicken stock slowly while constantly stirring.
2. Strain the mixture so you can remove any air bubbles. Pour in a baking dish and cover with aluminum foil.
3. Place the trivet into the bottom of the instant pot and add one cup of water.
4. Set the baking dish into the pot and seal the lid into place. Set pot on low pressure for six minutes.
5. Naturally release the pressure.
6. Carefully take the dish out and remove the tin foil. Garnish with green onions if you so choose to.
7. Mix the water, soy sauce, and fish sauce together and pour on top.
8. Serve warm.

08 Cheesy Egg Bake

Prep Time: 5 minutes; **Cook Time**: 15 minutes

Recommended Serving Size: ½ cup; **Serves**: 4

Ingredients:

- 6 slices chopped bacon
- ½ cup shredded cheese of choice
- ¼ cup milk
- 6 eggs
- 2 cups frozen hash browns

Directions:

1. The bacon should first be chopped into small pieces and then cook in the instant pot until crispy.
2. You can add any vegetables you would like at this point and sauté until tender.
3. Add the hash browns and let them thaw slightly.
4. Grease an oven proof baking dish that fits inside the instant pot.
5. Whisk together the eggs, pepper, salt, cheese, and milk in a bowl and add the bacon and hash browns.
6. Pour the egg mixture into the prepared container.
7. Pour one and a half cups of water into the instant pot and set the trivet inside. Put the baking dish on top of the trivet.

8. Place on the lid and seal. Cook the dish on high for ten minutes.

9. Once done, use the quick release function to get rid of the pressure.

10. Carefully take out the dish and invert onto a plate. You may need to run a knife around the edges to loosen.

11. Serve with garnishes of your choice or extra cheese.

09 Quiche

Prep Time: 10 minutes; **Cook Time**: 40 minutes

Recommended Serving Size: 1 slice; **Serves**: 4

Ingredients:

- 2 tbsp. chopped chives
- 1 cup shredded cheese of choice
- 1 cup water
- ½ cup milk
- 6 large eggs

Directions:

1. Set the trivet insert into your instant pot and add in the water.
2. Wrap a 7-inch spring form pan with aluminum foil. Let some hang over the top to make a sling for easy removal. Spray the pan with cooking spray.
3. Whisk the pepper, salt, chives, milk, and eggs together.
4. Place the cheese in the bottom of the pan. Pour the egg mixture over the cheese.
5. Set the pan in on the trivet. Close and seal on the lid. Set to high and cook for 30 minutes.
6. Once done, wait ten minutes. Then do a quick release for the remaining pressure.

7. Open the lid, take out the pan, and it allow cool slightly before removing the quiche from the pan.

8. Slice and serve.

9. Leftovers can be stored in airtight container and reheated in microwave.

10 Meat Lovers Quiche

Prep Time: 5 minutes; **Cook Time**: 40 minutes

Recommended Serving Size: 1 slice; **Serves**: 4

Ingredients:

- 6 large eggs
- 2 large green onions, chopped
- ½ cup milk
- 1 cup shredded cheese
- Favorite breakfast meats

Directions:

1. Set the trivet insert into the instant pop. Add in a cup of water.

2. Whisk together the pepper, salt, and eggs. Add in meats of choice, cheese, and onions. Whisk together. Pour mixture into a baking dish that has been greased with nonstick spray.

3. Cover the dish with foil. Make a foil sling to wrap around the dish to ease it into the instant pot. Close and seal the lid. Place on high and cook for 30 minutes. Once done, turn off the pot, and wait for ten minutes then use the quick release.

4. Open the lid carefully and remove the dish. Sprinkle with more cheese if desired.

5. Serve and enjoy.

11 Cheesy Bacon Hashbrowns

Prep Time: 0 minutes; **Cook Time**: 3 hours

Recommended Serving Size: 1 cup; **Serves**: 4

Ingredients:

- ½ chopped onion
- 16 oz. sour cream
- 1 pkg. frozen hash browns
- ¼ cup milk
- 1 can cream of mushroom soup

Directions:

1. Thaw the hash browns slightly.
2. Combine the milk, sour cream, onion, soup, and hash browns. Season with some pepper, garlic, and salt.
3. Set the instant pot on sauté. Put some butter in the bottom of the instant pot and allow it to melt. Swirl so it coats the instant pot.
4. Pour the hash brown mixture into the instant pot. Sprinkle with cheese.
5. Close lid and seal.
6. Set to slow cook on high. Cook for 3 hours.
7. Once done, quick release the pressure.
8. Sprinkle with some cooked bacon and enjoy.

12 Peaches and Cream Oatmeal

Prep Time: 0 minutes; **Cook Time**: 13 minutes

Recommended Serving Size: 1 cup; **Serves**: 4

Ingredients:

- 1 tsp. vanilla
- 4 cups water
- 1 chopped peach
- 2 cups rolled oats

Directions:

1. Place the vanilla, peaches, water, and oats to the instant pot.
2. Close the lid and seal in place.
3. Set to porridge on high for three minutes
4. Once the time is up, allow the pressure to release on its own for ten minutes.
5. Use the quick release function to get rid of any remaining pressure.
6. Equally, divide among four bowls.

13 Cinnamon Banana Oatmeal

Prep Time: 20 minutes; **Cook Time**: 5 minutes

Recommended Serving Size: 1 cup; **Serves**: 3

Ingredients:

- 1 c old fashioned oatmeal
- 1 tbsp. brown sugar
- 1 c water
- 2 bananas
- 1 c milk

Directions:

1. Coat the inside of your instant pot with some cooking spray. Add the water, milk, and oatmeal.
2. Slice one banana and place it in the pot. Add the brown sugar and a sprinkle of cinnamon. Give everything a good stir.
3. Close the lid and seal.
4. Set to manual for five minutes.
5. When timer beeps, allow the pot to sit for 10 minutes as the pressure releases naturally. Use the quick release function for any remaining pressure.
6. Stir the oatmeal and spoon into bowls.
7. Slice the other banana and serve with oatmeal.

14 Maple Brown Sugar Oatmeal

Prep Time: 5 minutes; **Cook Time**: 8 hours

Recommended Serving Size: 1 cup; **Serves**: 12

Ingredients:

- 6 to 8 cups water
- 1 tsp. ground cinnamon
- ¼ c maple syrup
- 2 c steel cut oats
- ¼ c packed brown sugar

Directions:

1. Spray the instant pot with cooking spray.
2. Put all of the ingredients in and mix together.
3. Close the lid and seal.
4. Set to slow cook on low. Cook for eight hours.
5. When timer goes off, quick release pressure. Open the pot carefully.
6. Remove lid and stir well.
7. Serve with any other toppings or fruit of choice.

15 Pumpkin Coffee Cake Oatmeal

Prep Time: 0 minutes; **Cook Time**: 23 minutes

Recommended Serving Size: 1 cup; **Serves**: 6 to 8

Ingredients:

- 4 ½ cups water
- 1 ½ cups pumpkin puree
- 1 ½ steel cut oats
- 3 tsp. cinnamon
- 1 tsp. vanilla

Directions:

1. Put all of the ingredients into the instant pot.
2. Close the lid and seal.
3. Set to manual for three minutes.
4. When timer goes off, release pressure naturally for about 20 minutes. Open the pot carefully.
5. Stir everything together. Serve with a sprinkling of brown sugar, cinnamon, and pecans.

Main Course

16 Buffalo Chicken

Prep Time: 0 minutes; **Cook Time**: 15 minutes

Recommended Serving Size: 1 cup; **Serves**: 4

Ingredients:

- 12 ounces buffalo sauce
- 3 pounds chicken breast
- 1 packet ranch dressing mix

Directions:

1. Place all of the ingredients into the instant pot.
2. Cover with lid and seal. Set on poultry for 15 minutes. Quick release the pressure once done
3. Shred the chicken and serve.

17 Pulled Pork

Prep Time: 5 minutes; **Cook Time**: 2 hours, 12 minutes

Recommended Serving Size: 1 cup; **Serves**: 12

Ingredients:

- 2 cups barbecue sauce, divided
- 2 tbsp. vegetable oil
- 4 pounds pork shoulder, boneless, halved
- ½ cup water

Directions:

1. Heat the oil on the sauté setting. Cook the pork one half at a time. Brown each side for three minutes. Set on a plate once browned. Once done, add ½ cup of water and half of the barbecue sauce in and mix together well. Place the pork back in the instant pot.

2. Place the instant pot on high for 75 minutes. Once finished, allow the pressure to release completely naturally. This should take around 20 minutes. Take out the meat and shred. Throw out any fat. Strain the juices from pot. Reserve ½ cup of the juices.

3. Add the shredded pork, ½ cup cooking liquid, and the rest of the barbecue sauce to pot. Stir well to combine. Place on sauté setting until it begins to simmer. Serve with crusty bread or rolls when finished.

18 Turkey Legs

Prep Time: 0 minutes; **Cook Time**: 8 hours

Recommended Serving Size: 1 leg; **Serves**: 6

Ingredients:

- 6 turkey legs
- 6 – 12 X 16-inch foil squares
- 3 tsp. poultry seasoning, divided
- Pepper
- Salt

Directions:

1. Clean each of the turkey legs and dry. Season with ½ tsp poultry seasoning, salt, and pepper. Wrap each seasoned leg with foil.

2. Place the legs into the instant pot.

3. Set on the lowest setting for slow cooker, and cook for eight hours.

4. Quick pressure release once done.

19 Sirloin Tips with Gravy

Prep Time: 10 minutes; **Cook Time**: 50 minutes

Recommended Serving Size: 1 cup; **Serves**: 12

Ingredients:

- 5 pounds sirloin tip roast, cubed
- 1 large, diced onion
- 3 tbsp. vegetable oil, divided
- 2 cups beef broth
- Slurry made with ½ cup flour and 1 ½ cups water

Directions:

1. Set the instant pot to the sauté function. Add one tablespoon of oil. When hot, place meat in a single layer on the bottom. You will need to brown the meat in batches. Place on a plate when each batch is finished. When all the meat is finished, put the onion in and cook for about five minutes, or until it becomes soft.

2. Put meat back into the pot with the broth. Seal the lid in place and cook for 15 minutes on high. Once finished, use quick pressure release. Whisk the flour and water together until no lumps remain. Stir into the meat and set on sauté. Let the mixture come to a boil, continuously stirring until broth has thickened.

3. Taste test and adjust seasonings if needed.

20 Salmon

Prep Time: 5 minutes; **Cook Time**: 1 hour, 5 minutes

Recommended Serving Size: 1 piece; **Serves**: Varies

Ingredients:

- Sliced lemon
- 1 pound salmon, skin on
- 1 cup liquid of choice
- Favorite herbs and spices
- Slice onion

Directions:

1. Slice the salmon into servings sizes. Sprinkle with you spices of choice.

2. Line the instant pot with foil or parchment paper.

3. Set the aromatic ingredients on the bottom of your pot. Lay the salmon on top. Add in the liquid. This needs to almost cover the salmon.

4. Seal the lid into place. Set to low and cook for one hour. This will vary depending on the salmon size. Remove salmon by lifting out the foil.

21 Lamb Ribs

Prep Time: 5 minutes; **Cook Time**: 10 hours

Recommended Serving Size: 2 ribs; **Serves**: 6

Ingredients:

- 5 cloves minced garlic
- Dash thyme
- 1 pound lamb spare ribs
- Pepper and salt
- 1 tsp. extra virgin olive oil

Directions:

1. Put the thyme, pepper, and salt on the ribs, and rub. Put the ribs in the instant pot. Place the other ingredients on top.

2. Turn to slow cooker setting on high for two hours.

3. Turn heat to low and cook for another eight hours.

4. When finished, use natural pressure release.

22 Kalua Pork

Prep Time: 5 minutes; **Cook Time**: 2 hours, 20 minutes

Recommended Serving Size: 1 cup; **Serves**: 6

Ingredients:

- 1 tbsp. Hickory flavored liquid smoke
- 2 tbsp. oil
- 4 pounds pork shoulder or butt roast, halved
- ½ cup water
- 2 tbsp. salt

Directions:

1. Set instant pot to sauté setting. Put the oil in the pot. When hot, brown the pork. You will need to brown each half separately. Cook for three minutes on each side. Set on plate and cook the rest of the meat.

2. Turn off cooker and add the water and liquid smoke to the pot. Mix well and place meat back in. Sprinkle with some salt.

3. Cook on high pressure for 90 minutes. When finished, use natural pressure release. This will take about 20 minutes. When the valve is completely down, remove the lid. Take pork out of cooker and place in a large bowl. Shred the meat, getting rid of any fat. Take some juice from pot and add to meat to keep it moist.

4. Serve over mashed potatoes or rice.

23 Steak

Prep Time: 0 minutes; **Cook Time**: 35 minutes

Recommended Serving Size: 8 ounces; **Serves**: 4

Ingredients:

- 2-pound flank steak
- 1 tbsp. Worcestershire sauce
- ½ cup oil
- 2 tbsp. onion soup mix
- 4 tbsp. apple cider vinegar

Directions:

1. Set the instant pot to sauté.
2. When hot, brown the steak on both sides.
3. Mix the Worcestershire, oil, onion soup mix, and vinegar together. Pour over the steak.
4. Close the lid and seal.
5. Set to meat and cook for 35 minutes.
6. Use quick pressure release.

24 Salt Baked Chicken

Prep Time: 5 minutes; **Cook Time**: 40 minutes

Recommended Serving Size: 2 legs; **Serves**: 4

Ingredients:

- Salt
- Pepper
- 8 chicken legs
- ¼ tsp. five spice powder
- 2 tsp. dried ginger

Directions:

1. Coat the chicken with the ginger, salt, spice powder, and pepper.
2. Wrap the chicken in parchment paper.
3. Place the chicken in a shallow dish that will fit in the instant pot.
4. Put in the steamer rack, and add one cup of water.
5. Place the dish on the steamer rack.
6. Set on high, and cook for 20 minutes.
7. Release pressure naturally, about 20 minutes.

25 Filipino Chicken Adobo

Prep Time: 0 minutes; **Cook Time**: 15 minutes

Recommended Serving Size: 2 thighs; **Serves**: 2

Ingredients:

- 2 pounds chicken thighs
- 1 bay leaf
- 2 cloves crushed garlic
- ¼ cup soy sauce
- ¼ cup white vinegar

Directions:

1. Set the instant pot to poultry.
2. Put all ingredients in the pot.
3. Seal the lid on. Set on high for 15 minutes.
4. Use the pressure quick release.

26 Salsa Verde Chicken

Prep Time: 0 minutes; **Cook Time**: 25 minutes

Recommended Serving Size: ½ cup; **Serves**: 4

Ingredients:

- 8 ounce salsa Verde
- ½ tsp. cumin
- ½ tsp. salt
- 1 pound boneless chicken breast
- ½ tsp. paprika

Directions:

1. Place all of the ingredients in the instant pot.
2. Seal the lid into place.
3. Set to cook on high for 25 minutes.
4. When finished, use the quick pressure release.
5. Take the chicken out and shred it. Mix the chicken back in and enjoy.

27 Sous Vide Duck

Prep Time: 2 hours; **Cook Time**: 38 minutes

Recommended Serving Size: 1 breast; **Serves**: 2

Ingredients:

- 1 tsp salt
- 2 tsp minced garlic
- 1/3 tsp thyme
- 2 boneless duck breasts
- 1 tbsp. vegetable oil

Directions:

1. Rub the spices into the duck breast. Place it in the refrigerator for two hours.
2. Rinse the spices off of the duck.
3. Place the duck into a Ziploc bag and remove as much air as possible.
4. Put water in the instant pot up to the seven cup mark.
5. Switch the pot to warm. Allow it to sit for 20 minutes.
6. Place the bag in the water. Leave for 38 minutes.
7. Remove the bag, and dry the breasts.
8. Turn the pot to sauté. Add the oil to the pot. Once the oil is hot, sear the skin of the duck. Flip and cook about 20 seconds more.

28 Leg of Lamb

Prep Time: 5 minutes; **Cook Time**: 10 hours

Recommended Serving Size: 1 cup; **Serves**: 4

Ingredients:

- 4 pounds leg of lamb, rolled
- 2 cloves minced garlic
- 1 packet onion soup mix
- ½ cup soy sauce
- 1 onion sliced

Directions:

1. Place all of the ingredients in your instant pot. Stir to combine.
2. Add enough water to cover the leg of lamb.
3. Set to slow cook on low for 10 hours.
4. Once done, use the quick release function to remove all of the pressure.
5. Take the lamb out and allow it to rest before slicing. Enjoy.

29 Cream Cheese Chicken

Prep Time: 0 minutes; **Cook Time**: 15 minutes

Recommended Serving Size: 1 cup; **Serves**: 4

Ingredients:

- 4 ounces cream cheese
- 1 pound chicken
- 1 packet Italian dressing mix
- 1 can cream of chicken soup

Directions:

1. Put all of the ingredients in the pot. Seal the lid on.
2. Set to the poultry setting. Cook for 15 minutes. Let the pressure release naturally.

30 Chile Verde

Prep Time: 0 minutes; **Cook Time**: 25 minutes

Recommended Serving Size: 1 cup; **Serves**: 6

Ingredients:

- 2 cups green salsa
- 2 pounds pork, cut into pieces

Directions:

1. Set the instant pot to sauté. Place the pork in even layer on the bottom and allow to brown.

2. Add the salsa. Close and seal on the lid.

3. Set the pot to meat/stew for 25 minutes.

4. Once done, use the quick pressure release function to remove the pressure.

5. Take out the pork, shred it, and mix it back in.

6. Serve over rice.

31 Ranch Pork Chops

Prep Time: 0 minutes; **Cook Time**: 15 minutes

Recommended Serving Size: 1 chop; **Serves**: 2

Ingredients:

- 1 can cream of chicken soup
- 2/3 cup water
- 1 pound boneless pork chops
- 1 ranch dressing packet

Directions:

1. Place all of the above ingredients into your instant pot, and seal the lid on.

2. Set the pot to meat/stew setting for 15 minutes.

3. Once done, use the quick release function to get rid of all the pressure.

32 Maple Mustard Chicken

Prep Time: 0 minutes; **Cook Time**: 10 minutes

Recommended Serving Size: 1 cup; **Serves**: 2

Ingredients:

- 3 tbsp. stone ground mustard
- 1 tbsp. quick tapioca
- 1 pound chicken breast
- ¼ cup maple syrup
- ¼ cup water

Directions:

1. Put the chicken in the pot.
2. Mix the syrup, mustard, tapioca, and water together.
3. Pour this mixture over the chicken.
4. Close and seal on the lid.
5. Set to the poultry setting for 10 minutes.
6. Quick release the pressure.

33 Beef Short Ribs

Prep Time: 30 minutes; **Cook Time**: 38 minutes

Recommended Serving Size: 1 cup; **Serves**: 2 to 4

Ingredients:

- Dry rub
- 1 pound beef short ribs
- 1 cup water
- ½ cup barbecue sauce

Directions:

1. Rub the ribs with the dry rub. Place them in the refrigerator for 30 minutes.
2. Set the trivet insert into your instant pot. Add in one cup of water, and set the ribs in on the trivet
3. Close the lid and seal.
4. Set the pot to manual for 28 minutes.
5. Once done, give the pot 15 minutes to release the pressure naturally.
6. Open carefully and place the ribs on a baking sheet.
7. Baste the ribs with the barbecue sauce. Broil them for three minutes.
8. Serve and enjoy.

34 Three Packet Roast

Prep Time: 15 minutes; **Cook Time**: 1 hour, 20 minutes

Recommended Serving Size: 1 cup; **Serves**: 12

Ingredients:

- 1 packet ranch dressing mix
- 2 cups water
- 1 packet Italian dressing mix
- 3-pound chuck roast
- 1 packet brown gravy mix

Directions:

1. Trim the chuck roast of any excess fat. Place it in the bottom of the instant pot.
2. Mix all of the seasoning packets together in the water. Place this mixture over the roast.
3. Close the lid and seal.
4. Set to manual for one hour.
5. It will take the pot about 15 minutes to reach full pressure, and then the roast will cook for one hour.
6. When timer goes off, release the pressure naturally for about 20 minutes. Open pot carefully.
7. Remove the lid and shred the meat.
8. Serve any way you would like.

35 Beef Barbecue

Prep Time: 15 minutes; **Cook Time**: 75 minutes
Recommended Serving Size: 1/3 cup; **Serves**: 9

Ingredients:

- 1 1/3 lb Angus roast, frozen
- 1 ½ cup favorite BBQ sauce
- 1 c water

Directions:

1. Spray the instant pot with cooking spray.
2. Add the water and roast to the pot.
3. Close the lid and seal.
4. Set to meat for 70 minutes.
5. Once done, use the quick release function to get rid of the pressure, and then turn the pot off
6. Take the meat out. Trim off any skin or fat your see and, shred. Discard any other fat you come across.
7. Empty water out of the instant pot.
8. Place the beef back into the pot, and pour the barbecue sauce over the top.
9. Set the pot to sauté. Stir everything together as it heats.
10. Let the mixture cook for three minutes.
11. Serve as you want.

36 Orange Chicken

Prep Time: 5 minutes; **Cook Time**: 3 hours

Recommended Serving Size: 1 chicken breast; **Serves**: 4

Ingredients:

- 1/8 tsp red pepper flakes
- 2 cups orange sauce
- 4 boneless, skinless chicken breasts

Directions:

1. Spray the instant pot with cooking spray.
2. Place all ingredients into the bottom of the instant pot.
3. Close and seal lid.
4. Set on slow cook and high for three hours. Once done, quick release pressure.
5. Carefully remove chicken and shred with two forks.
6. Serve over rice and enjoy.

37 French Onion Pork Chops

Prep Time: 5 minutes; **Cook Time**: 4 hours

Recommended Serving Size: 1 pork chop; **Serves**: 4

Ingredients:

- ½ cup sour cream
- 1 can French onion soup
- 1 can chicken broth
- 4 boneless pork chops

Directions:

1. Pour chicken broth into the bottom of the instant pot. Add pork chops.
2. Close and seal lid.
3. Set on slow cook.
4. Set on high and cook for three and a half hours.
5. When finished, quick release the pressure. Drain the juices out of the instant pot.
6. Mix the sour cream and French onion soup together. Stir well to combine.
7. Pour over the pork chops, turning to coat.
8. Turn the pot to sauté. Simmer for about 30 minutes until warmed through.
9. Serve with favorite side.

38 Santé Fe Chicken

Prep Time: 5 minutes; **Cook Time**: 3 hours, 30 minutes

Recommended Serving Size: 1 cup; **Serves**: 4

Ingredients:

- 1 7 oz can diced green chilies
- 2 cans fiesta nacho soup
- ½ sliced onion
- 4 boneless, skinless chicken breasts

Directions:

1. Place all the ingredients in the bottom of the instant pot.
2. Close and seal lid.
3. Set to slow cook.
4. Set on high and cook for three hours.
5. When finished, quick release pressure.
6. Carefully remove chicken and shred. Place chicken back into the instant pot.
7. Turn to sauté and let chicken reheat for about 30 minutes. Enjoy.

One Pot Meals

39 BBQ Wings

Prep Time: 0 minutes; **Cook Time**: 50 minutes

Recommended Serving Size: 6 to 8 wings; **Serves**: 2

Ingredients:

- 1 cup cold tap water
- ½ cup barbecue sauce
- 2 pounds chicken wings

Directions:

1. Add the water to the instant pot. Add in the rack insert, and arrange the chicken on top of the rack and close the lid. Set on high for five minutes. Once done, let the pressure release naturally.

2. While waiting, set the oven to 450°F. When the wings are finished cooking, pat them dry. Place the chicken in a big mixing bowl, and then toss with some barbecue sauce. Lay them on a baking tray with a wire rack.

3. Bake about 8 to 15 minutes, or until the sauce is glossy and caramelized.

40 Barbecue Beef Sandwiches

Prep Time: 5 minutes; **Cook Time**: 40 minutes

Recommended Serving Size: ½ cup; **Serves**: 6

Ingredients:

- Buns
- 2-pound beef roast
- 1 cup barbecue sauce

Directions:

1. Clean the roast of any excess fat that you can see. Place the meat and sauce in the instant pot.
2. Close the lid and seal.
3. Set on meat for 40 minutes.
4. Use the pressure quick release once they are done.
5. Take the meat out and shred.
6. Place the meat on buns and enjoy.

41 Lasagna Pie

Prep Time: 0 minutes; **Cook Time**: 30 minutes

Recommended Serving Size: ¼ section; **Serves**: 4

Ingredients:

- Italian sausage, ground
- Dry lasagna noodles
- Shredded parmesan
- Jar pasta sauce
- Ricotta

Directions:

1. Spray a springform pan with nonstick spray. Place a layer of noodles in the bottom.
2. Add the ricotta and sauce, and spread evenly.
3. Add the sausage and shredded cheese.
4. Place another layer of noodles and repeat the process until no ingredients remain.
5. Cover the pan with foil.
6. Put the trivet in the instant pot, and add 1 ½ cups of water to the pot.
7. Place the lasagna on the trivet.
8. Set to high for 20 minutes.

9. When finished, release pressure naturally for about 20 minutes.

10. Carefully remove the pan from the pot and ease the lasagna out of the pan. Slice and serve.

42 Barbacoa de Cordero

Prep Time: 30 minutes; **Cook Time**: 36 minutes

Recommended Serving Size: 1 cup; **Serves**: 4

Ingredients:

- 2 tbsp. oil
- 2 pounds lamb shoulder
- 16 ounce can enchilada sauce
- 2 small onions, chopped
- 2 cloves minced garlic

Directions:

1. Marinate the lamb in the enchilada sauce for at least 30 minutes.
2. Set the instant pot to sauté, and pour in the oil.
3. After the oil has heated, place in the onions and sauté them until they are softened. Add the garlic.
4. Put the lamb and enchilada sauce in the pot, and let the mixture come to a boil.
5. Set pot to the stew setting for 36 minutes.
6. Once done, remove the lamb and shred.
7. Serve as you would like.

43 Chicken Soup

Prep Time: 10 minutes; **Cook Time**: 1 hour

Recommended Serving Size: 1 cup; **Serves**: 6

Ingredients:

- 2 boneless chicken breasts
- 2 large, chopped carrot
- 2 small diced onion
- 4 cups water
- 4 diced potatoes

Directions:

1. Place everything into your pot. Add some pepper and salt and cook on manual for 35 minutes.
2. Once finished, release the pressure naturally. Normally about 15 minutes. Then do a quick release for the remaining pressure.

44 Duck a l'Orange

Prep Time: 5 minutes; **Cook Time**: 10 hours

Recommended Serving Size: 1 breasts; **Serves**: 2

Ingredients:

- 2 duck breasts, sliced in half
- 1 onion, cut into eighths
- 2 oranges, peeled and sliced
- 1 can orange juice concentrate
- 1 apple, sliced

Directions:

1. Season the duck with pepper and salt.
2. Put the duck in the instant pot followed by the oranges, apples and the onion.
3. Pour the orange juice over everything.
4. Set to slow cook on low for 10 hours.
5. Once done, use the quick release function to get rid of the pressure.
6. Take the duck out and get rid of all the excess liquid.

45 Pot Roast

Prep Time: 0 minutes; **Cook Time**: 35 minutes

Recommended Serving Size: 1 cup; **Serves**: 4

Ingredients:

- 3 cups potatoes
- 1 cup water
- 2 2/3 cup chunked carrots
- 1 packet onion soup mix
- 1 pound beef chuck

Directions:

1. Place the roast in the instant pot.
2. In a separate bowl, mix together the soup and water.
3. Pour this mixture over top of the beef.
4. Put the vegetables in the pot around the beef.
5. Close and seal on the lid.
6. Set on meat/stew setting for 35 minutes.
7. Release the pressure carefully.

46 French Dip Sandwiches

Prep Time: 5 minutes; **Cook Time**: 35 minutes

Recommended Serving Size: 1 sandwich; **Serves**: 2

Ingredients:

- ½ tsp. minced garlic
- 2 pounds roast beef
- ½ tsp. beef bouillon
- 1 ½ tsp. rosemary
- 1/3 cup soy sauce

Directions:

1. Grab the roast and rim off any extra fat that you see, and place it in the pot.
2. Stir the soy sauce, bouillon, rosemary, and garlic together.
3. Pour this over the roast.
4. Add in water to cover the roast.
5. Close and seal on the lid.
6. Set to beef for 35 minutes. Release the pressure naturally.
7. Remove the beef and shred. Taste and add pepper and salt if you need.
8. Serve on buns.

47 Mexican Chicken in a Bowl

Prep Time: 5 minutes; **Cook Time**: 30 minutes

Recommended Serving Size: ½ cup; **Serves**: 4

Ingredients:

- 1 cup rice
- 1 can Rotel
- 2 cups water
- 1 ½ pounds chicken
- 1 can black beans

Directions:

1. Season the chicken with your favorite spices. Lay it in the bottom of the instant pot. Add one cup of water or broth. Place trivet on top.
2. Set a glass baking dish on top of the trivet.
3. Add the water, rice, black beans, and Rotel. Stir to combine.
4. Close the lid and seal.
5. Set to rice and cook for 12 minutes.
6. Release pressure naturally for 10 minutes.
7. When the ten minutes are up, release the rest of the pressure manually.
8. Carefully remove the glass dish and trivet.

48 Sausage and Cabbage

Prep Time: 5 minutes; **Cook Time**: 1 hour

Recommended Serving Size: ½ cup; **Serves**: 6

Ingredients:

- 2 packages smoked sausages
- 1 tsp minced garlic
- 1 small sliced onion
- ¼ cup water
- 1 small cabbage, cut into strips

Directions:

1. Set the pot to sauté. Pour the oil in the bottom. Add the onions and garlic.
2. Next, add the cabbage. Slice the sausages into circles and add to the pot.
3. Season with pepper and salt. Give everything a good stir.
4. Turn off sauté and put on manual for five minutes.
5. When the timer goes off, naturally release the pressure for ten minutes.
6. Manually release the rest of the pressure.

49 Healthy Mississippi Roast

Prep Time: 20 minutes; **Cook Time**: varies

Recommended Serving Size: 1 cup; **Serves**: 4

Ingredients:

- 1 packet ranch dressing mix
- 1 cup beef broth
- ½ jar banana pepper rings, hot if you like
- 3 to 4 pound chuck roast
- ½ stick butter

Directions:

1. Season the beef with pepper, salt, garlic, and half of the ranch packet. Let it sit for 20 minutes.
2. Pour the beef broth into the pot. Place the roast in. Sprinkle in the rest of the ranch packet.
3. Place all of the butter over the top.
4. Place the lid on and seal it into place. Set on manual for 22 minutes per pound of beef.
5. When the timer goes off, naturally release the pressure for 15 minutes. Manually release the rest of the pressure.
6. Open the lid. Shred the beef.

50 Cheesy Tortellini

Prep Time: 5 minutes; **Cook Time**: 10 hours

Recommended Serving Size: 1 breasts; **Serves**: 2

Ingredients:

- 2 tsp. basil
- 1 pkg. refrigerated cheese tortellini
- ½ tsp. garlic powder
- 1 jar pasta sauce of choice
- 4 cups mozzarella cheese

Directions:

1. Spray the instant pot with nonstick spray.
2. Add half of the pasta sauce to the bottom of your instant pot.
3. Place the tortellini in an even layer over the sauce.
4. Sprinkle with garlic powder, and evenly add two cups of cheese.
5. Add the remaining paste sauce over the cheese layer.
6. Put the remaining tortellini in another even layer, and sprinkle with the remaining cheese.
7. Sprinkle on the basil.
8. Set to slow cook on high for 1 hour 30 minutes.
9. Once done, quick release the pressure.

51 Pulled Pork Sandwiches

Prep Time: 20 minutes; **Cook Time**: 6 hours, 30 minutes

Recommended Serving Size: 1 sandwich; **Serves**: 8

Ingredients:

- 1 can Dr. Pepper
- 3 pounds pork tenderloin
- 1 ounce bottle barbecue sauce
- Buns

Directions:

1. Cut the tenderloin in half and put both pieces into the instant pot.
2. Mix the barbecue sauce and Dr. Pepper together and pour over the pork.
3. Close and seal the lid.
4. Set to slow cook on low for six and a half hours.
5. When done, use the quick release function to get rid of the pressure.
6. Take the pork out and shred, discarding all fat.
7. Place the pork on hamburger buns.
8. Serve with coleslaw if desired.

52 Lentil Tacos

Prep Time: 0 minutes; **Cook Time**: 15 minutes

Recommended Serving Size: 1 taco; **Serves**: 4

Ingredients:

- ½ tsp. cumin
- 2 cups dry brown lentils
- 4 ounces tomato sauce
- 4 cups water

Directions:

1. Put all the ingredients into your pot and mix everything together well. Season with the onion powder, garlic powder, chili powder, pepper, and salt. Mix everything together.
2. Close and seal the lid.
3. Set to manual for 15 minutes.
4. Once done, turn off and use the quick release function to remove the pressure.
5. Carefully open the lid and give the mixture a stir. Let it sit a few minutes.
6. Serve with either soft or hard tacos or as a taco salad.

53 Instant Rice Dinner

Prep Time: 0 minutes; **Cook Time**: 20 minutes

Recommended Serving Size: 1 cup; **Serves**: 4

Ingredients:

- 3 slices bacon cut up
- Leftover veggies
- 1 cup rice
- Leftover meat
- 1 cup bruschetta

Directions:

1. Your instant pot should be set to the sauté function. Pour in the oil and heat. Place the bacon into the hot pot and let it cook for about five minutes.

2. Mix in the leftover meat and sauté with the bacon for another five minutes.

3. Mix the rice in and cook it with everything for a few more minutes.

4. Add a cup of water, bruschetta, and vegetables.

5. Close the lid and seal.

6. Set to manual for five minutes.

7. Once done, let the mixture sit another five minutes. Then release the pressure.

54 Pina Colada Chicken

Prep Time: 15 minutes; **Cook Time**: 15 minutes

Recommended Serving Size: 1 cup; **Serves**: 4

Ingredients:

- 2 tbsp. coconut aminos
- 2 pounds chicken thighs
- 1 tsp cinnamon
- 1 cup pineapple chunks
- ½ cup full fat coconut cream

Directions:

1. Place all the ingredients in the instant pot.
2. Close the lid and seal.
3. Set to poultry for 15 minutes.
4. Once done, naturally release the pressure for ten minutes.
5. Open and remove the chicken.
6. Stir everything together. Serve the chicken with the sauce and sliced green onions.

55 White Chicken Chili

Prep Time: 5 minutes; **Cook Time**: 15 minutes

Recommended Serving Size: 1 cup; **Serves**: 12

Ingredients:

- 6 cups chicken broth
- 2 cans great northern beans
- 2 skinless, boneless chicken breasts
- 2 cups salsa Verde
- 2 tsp. ground cumin

Directions:

1. Place all of the ingredients, minus the beans, into your instant pot and mix everything together.
2. Close the lid and seal.
3. Set to slow cook on low for 8 hours.
4. Once done, use the quick release function to remove the pressure.
5. Take the chicken out and shred. Once shredded mix the chicken back in. Add the beans and seal the lid back into place. Set your pot to the high setting for ten minutes.
6. Use the quick release for the pressure again, and stir everything together.

56 Sloppy Joes

Prep Time: 10 minutes; **Cook Time**: 2 hours, 30 minutes

Recommended Serving Size: 1 sandwich; **Serves**: 4

Ingredients:

- 4 hamburger buns
- ½ tsp garlic salt
- ¾ cup chopped white onion
- 1 can sloppy joe sauce
- 1 lb ground beef

Directions:

1. Turn the instant pot to sauté setting. When heated, place the garlic salt, chopped onions, and ground beef in the bottom. Cook until the meat is no longer pink and onions are soft. Drain.
2. Add the sloppy joe sauce to the drained meat mixture and stir to combine.
3. Close and seal lid.
4. Set on slow cook. Set on high and cook for two and a half hours.
5. When finished, quick release the pressure. Give it another stir.
6. Serve on hamburger buns.

57 Broccoli and Beef

Prep Time: 10 minutes; **Cook Time**: 1 hour, 30 minutes

Recommended Serving Size: 1 cup; **Serves**: 4

Ingredients:

- ¼ cup water
- 1 packet broccoli beef sauce
- 1 bag frozen broccoli florets
- 1 ½ lbs flank steak, fat trimmed

Directions:

1. Cut the flank steak into ½-inch strips going against the grain.
2. Now, cut the strips into two to three inch pieces.
3. Place on the bottom of the instant pot. Spread out so they are in an even layer.
4. Pour the water over the steak.
5. Close and seal lid.
6. Set to slow cook. Set on high and cook for one and a half hours until the meat is tender.
7. When finished, quick release the pressure and carefully drain the juices.
8. Put meat back into the instant pot and add the broccoli beef sauce and frozen broccoli. Stir to coat.

9. Turn the pot to sauté. Heat to boil and allow the broccoli to get warmed through.

10. Serve as is or over cooked rice.

Grains

58 Copycat Cilantro Lime Rice

Prep Time: 0 minutes; **Cook Time**: 10 minutes

Recommended Serving Size: 1 cup; **Serves**: 2

Ingredients:

- 1 tbsp. fresh lime juice

- 1 cup white rice

- 2 tbsp. vegetable oil

- 3 tbsp. fresh chopped cilantro

- 1 ¼ cups water

Directions:

1. Mix the rice and the water together in the instant pot and stir to combine. Mix in some salt. Set to high pressure and cook for three minutes. When the timer goes off, use natural pressure release for seven minutes. Use quick release to get rid of the remaining pressure. Use a fork to fluff up the rice.

2. Mix the lime juice, cilantro, and oil in a different bowl. Whisk well and mix into the rice. Tossing to combine.

59 Khichdi Dal

Prep Time: 0 minutes; **Cook Time**: 10 minutes

Recommended Serving Size: 1 cup; **Serves**: 4

Ingredients:

- 2 cups water
- ¼ tsp. salt
- 1 cup khichdi mix
- 1 tsp. Balti seasoning
- 1 tbsp. butter

Directions:

1. Rinse the Khichdi. Set the instant pot to sauté and place the butter in, allowing it to melt. Mix in the Balti seasoning. Cook for a minute. Add the Khichdi mix, water, and salt. Allow to boil and then seal on the lid.

2. Set the pot to rice for 10 minutes. Release the pressure naturally. Fluff.

60 Coffee Can Bread

Prep Time: 0 minutes; **Cook Time**: 25 minutes

Recommended Serving Size: 2 slices; **Serves**: Varies

Ingredients:

- 2 tbsp. flour
- Personal bread recipe or store bought bread mix
- Coffee can
- Cooking spray

Directions:

1. Prepare your bread according to your recipe.
2. Grease and flour the coffee can. Roll the bread into a dough ball the will fit in your can and place inside the can. Place tin foil over the top of the can. Allow the bread to rise.
3. Put the can in the instant pot. Add water to the pot until it comes about halfway up the can.
4. Set on high for 15 minutes.
5. Allow it to cool for about ten minutes, and then use the quick release function to remove the remaining pressure. Carefully remove the bread from the can.

61 Basmati Rice

Prep Time: 0 minutes; **Cook Time**: 6 minutes

Recommended Serving Size: 1 cup; **Serves**: 4

Ingredients:

- 2 cups water
- 2 cups Indian basmati rice

Directions:

1. Add all of the rice and the water to your instant pot and mix them together well.

2. Set on high for six minutes. Once done, use the quick pressure release. Use a fork to fluff the rice.

62 Mexican Rice

Prep Time: 5 minutes; **Cook Time**: 15 minutes

Recommended Serving Size: 1 cup; **Serves**: 4

Ingredients:

- 2 cups long grain rice
- ½ cup green salsa
- 1 avocado
- 2 ½ cup broth
- 1 cup cilantro

Directions:

1. Add the rice and broth to the instant pot. Seal the lid. Set on high for three minutes.

2. Once finished, allow the pot to sit for about ten minutes, and then use the quick release to get rid of the remaining pressure

3. Fluff the rice and allow it to cool a bit.

4. Put the salsa, cilantro, and avocado in a blender. Pulse the ingredients together until they are creamy. Mix into the rice. Mix everything together. Season with pepper and salt.

63 Israeli Couscous

Prep Time: 0 minutes; **Cook Time**: 10 minutes

Recommended Serving Size: 1 cup; **Serves**: 10

Ingredients:

- 2 tbsp. butter
- 2 cups couscous
- 2 ½ cups chicken broth

Directions:

1. Set the instant pot to sauté. Add the butter and melt.
2. When melted add the couscous and broth.
3. Cook on high for five minutes.
4. Use quick release to get rid of the pressure.
5. Fluff the couscous with a fork and season with pepper and salt if needed.

64 Creamy Polenta

Prep Time: 1 minutes; **Cook Time**: 8 minutes

Recommended Serving Size: 1 cup; **Serves**: 2

Ingredients:

- 2 cups + 3 tbsp. milk
- 3 tbsp. butter
- ½ tsp salt
- ½ cup polenta

Directions:

1. Set the pot to sauté. Add two cups of milk, and let it come to a boil.
2. Mix the salt and polenta into the milk.
3. Close the lid and seal.
4. Set your pot to high for eight minutes.
5. Release the pressure with quick release. Stir in the remaining milk and butter.

65 Fusilli with Spinach

Prep Time: 0 minutes; **Cook Time**: 11 minutes

Recommended Serving Size: 1 cup; **Serves**: 8

Ingredients:

- 4 tbsp. butter, cubed
- ½ cup grated parmesan cheese
- 1 pound whole wheat fusilli pasta
- 4 cloves minced garlic
- 4 cups frozen chopped spinach, don't thaw

Directions:

1. Put the pasta in the instant pot.
2. Add five cups of water to cover the pasta. Add the spinach and garlic across the top.
3. Close the lid and seal.
4. Set the pot to manual for six minutes.
5. Once done, quick release the pressure.
6. Open, stir, and add the parmesan cheese, butter, pepper, and salt. Stir again.
7. Put the lid back on and allow to sit for five minutes.
8. Serve sprinkled with more parmesan cheese.

66 Multigrain Rice

Prep Time: 2 minutes; **Cook Time**: 70 minutes

Recommended Serving Size: 1 cup; **Serves**: 6 to 8

Ingredients:

- 3 ¾ cups water
- 3 cups wild, or brown rice, rinsed (or a combo)
- 2 tbsp. olive oil

Directions:

1. Combine the oil, water, and grains in the pot. Season with salt if desired.
2. Select multigrain for 65 minutes.
3. Once done, let it sit another 5 minutes, and then fluff with a fork.

67 Spanish Brown Rice

Prep Time: 0 minutes; **Cook Time**: 21 minutes

Recommended Serving Size: 1 cup; **Serves**: 6 to 8

Ingredients:

- 3 cups chicken stock
- 2 tbsp. tomato paste
- 1 medium chopped onion
- 2 cups long grain brown rice
- 4 cloves minced garlic

Directions:

1. Set the instant pot to sauté. Add a few tablespoons of oil. Once hot, place the onions in and let them cook until they become soft.

2. Place in the tomato paste and garlic. Stir. Add some oregano if desired. Sauté a few more minutes.

3. Put the rice in the pot. Stir to combine. Cook another few minutes. This deepens the flavor in the rice

4. Mix in the chicken stock.

5. Place the lid on and seal it into place.

6. Set to manual for 15 minutes.

7. Once done, naturally release the pressure.

8. Take the lid off and then use a fork to fluff the rice, and enjoy.

68 Raisin Butter Rice

Prep Time: 3 minutes; **Cook Time**: 12 minutes

Recommended Serving Size: 1 cup; **Serves**: 4

Ingredients:

- 3 cups wild rice
- ¼ cup salted butter
- ½ cup raisins
- 1 tsp. salt

Directions:

1. Wash the rice until the water runs clear, and place it in the instant pot.
2. Put everything else in the pot and cover with water.
3. Set the instant pot on rice for 12 minutes.
4. Once done, use the quick release to remove the pressure. Take off the lid and use a fork to fluff the rice
5. Serve warm.

69 Wheat Berries

Prep Time: 5 minutes; **Cook Time**: 30 minutes

Recommended Serving Size: 1 cup; **Serves**: 4

Ingredients:

- Pinch salt
- 1 cup wheat berries
- 3 cups water

Directions:

1. Add the salt, wheat berries, and water to the instant pot.
2. Close the lid and seal.
3. Set to manual for 30 minutes.
4. Once done, quick release the pressure.
5. Drain the wheat berries and enjoy.

70 Coconut Quinoa

Prep Time: 0 minutes; **Cook Time**: 3 hours

Recommended Serving Size: 1 cup; **Serves**: 6

Ingredients:

- 1 can coconut milk
- 1 can black beans
- 1 cup quinoa, rinsed
- 1 tsp coconut oil
- 1 tsp. sugar

Directions:

1. Place all the ingredients in the instant pot. Season with garlic powder and salt, and mix together
2. Close the lid and seal.
3. Set to slow cook on low for 3 hours.
4. Once done, quick release the pressure.

71 Quinoa Risotto

Prep Time: 5 minutes; **Cook Time**: 3 hours

Recommended Serving Size: 1 cup; **Serves**: 4

Ingredients:

- 2 ½ cups chicken broth
- 1 clove minced garlic
- ¾ cup diced onion
- 1/3 cup parmesan cheese
- 1 cup quinoa, rinsed

Directions:

1. Combine the onion, garlic, and two tablespoons butter. Microwave for five minutes, stirring every 90 seconds. Put the mixture in the instant pot.

2. Add the pepper, salt, broth, and quinoa. Stir to combine. You may add other veggies and ingredients at this point if you'd like.

3. Close the lid and seal.

4. Set to slow cook on high for 3 hours.

5. Once done, use the quick release function to remove the pressure.

6. Mix the parmesan into the food. Taste test and adjust any seasonings that you need to.

72 Parmesan Risotto

Prep Time: 5 minutes; **Cook Time**: 20 minutes

Recommended Serving Size: 1 cup; **Serves**: 4

Ingredients:

- 4 cups chicken broth
- 4 tbsp. butter
- 1 small diced onion
- 1 ½ cups Arborio rice
- 2 cloves minced garlic

Directions:

1. Set to sauté. Add the butter and melt. Mix the onions in and let them cook until they have become soft. Stir in the rice and the garlic and cook one more minute. Add one cup of broth. Cook about three minutes, or until the broth is absorbed.
2. Add three cups of broth, pepper, and salt. Sprinkle with some parmesan cheese.
3. Close the lid and seal.
4. Set to manual for ten minutes.
5. Once done, naturally release the pressure for ten minutes. Use the quick release function for the rest of the pressure
6. Take off the lid and ladle into bowls with desired garnishes.

73 Confetti Basmati Rice

Prep Time: 10 minutes; **Cook Time**: 13 minutes

Recommended Serving Size: 1 cup; **Serves**: 4 to 6

Ingredients:

- 1 chopped onion
- 2 cups Basmati rice
- ½ cup frozen peas
- 1 medium bell pepper, chopped
- 1 grated carrot

Directions:

1. Set the pot to sauté. Add enough oil to coat the pot. Mix the onion in and allow it to cook until it becomes soft.
2. Put the bell pepper and carrots in a four-cup measuring cup. Press into an even layer.
3. Add water until it reaches the three-cup mark.
4. Put the peas and rice into the pot. Season with pepper and salt, and mix.
5. Add in the water, carrots, and bell pepper. Mix again.
6. Close the lid and seal.
7. Set to high pressure for three minutes.
8. Once done, naturally release the pressure for ten minutes then quick release the rest.
9. Fluff with a fork and enjoy.

74 Creamy Rice Pudding

Prep Time: 5 minutes; **Cook Time**: 30 minutes

Recommended Serving Size: 1 cup; **Serves**: 4

Ingredients:

- 5 cups milk
- 2 eggs
- 1 cup half and half
- ¾ cup sugar
- 1 ½ cups Arborio rice

Directions:

1. Mix the rice, sugar, and milk in the instant pot. Sprinkle with a little salt.
2. Set to sauté. Stir until the sugar is dissolved and boiling.
3. Close the lid and seal.
4. Set to rice.
5. While the rice is cooking, mix the half and half and eggs together. Add the vanilla for flavoring if desired.
6. When rice is finished, press cancel, and allow to sit for 15 minutes.
7. Use the quick pressure function to remove the remaining pressure. Take the lid off, and add the egg mixture. Add the raisins if you want.

8. Set the pot to sauté, and let everything come to a boil. Turn the cooker off.

9. Serve any way you would like.

10. Pudding will thicken as it cools, so add extra milk if you need to.

Veggies

75 Sweet Carrots

Prep Time: 0 minutes; **Cook Time**: 15 minutes

Recommended Serving Size: 1 cup; **Serves**: 4

Ingredients:

- 2 tbsp. brown sugar
- 4 cups baby carrots
- 1 tbsp. butter
- ½ tsp salt
- 1 cup water

Directions:

1. Add the water, salt, butter, and brown sugar to the instant pot. Mix well to combine. Set to sauté and add the carrots; tossing to coat. Seal the lid into place.

2. Set on steam for 15 minutes. Once done, use the quick release function to remove the pressure, and take the lid off.

3. Set to sauté, and cook until all of the liquid has evaporated.

76 Sweet Potatoes

Prep Time: 0 minutes; **Cook Time**: 15 minutes

Recommended Serving Size: 1 cup; **Serves**: Varies

Ingredients:

- Olive oil
- Sweet potatoes
- ½ cup water

Directions:

1. Wash the potatoes and dry. Rub them with some oil and wrap in tin foil.

2. Put the water in the instant pot and set in the trivet. Place the potatoes on the trivet.

3. Close and seal the lid. Set to high for 15 minutes then quick release the pressure.

77 Spaghetti Squash

Prep Time: 10 minutes; **Cook Time**: 17 minutes

Recommended Serving Size: 1 cup; **Serves**: 4

Ingredients:

- Spaghetti squash
- 1 cup water

Directions:

1. Slice the squash in half, and get rid of all the seeds. Put the steamer basket in the pot. Add the water. Place the squash into the steamer basket.

2. Cover and seal. Set to cook on high for seven minutes. Once done, use the quick release function to remove the pressure. Carefully take the squash out and shred with a fork.

3. Serve with your favorite pasta sauce.

78 Creamed Corn

Prep Time: 0 minutes; **Cook Time**: 2 hours

Recommended Serving Size: 1 cup; **Serves**: 2

Ingredients:

- 4 ounce cream cheese
- 2 tbsp. butter
- ½ cup milk
- 1 pound corn kernels
- 1 tsp. sugar

Directions:

1. Place the corn and sugar in the pot, and sprinkle with salt. Add the milk. Dot over with some cream cheese and butter

2. Place the lid on and lock. Set to high pressure for two hours.

3. Once done, use the quick release function to remove the pressure, and carefully take off the lid. Mix well.

4. If it's too thick, add more milk.

5. Taste test and add pepper and salt if needed.

79 Butternut Squash

Prep Time: 0 minutes; **Cook Time**: Varies

Recommended Serving Size: 1 cup; **Serves**: 6

Ingredients:

- Butternut squash
- 1 cup water

Directions:

1. Put the rack in the instant pot and fill with one cup of water. Wash the squash and cut into sections if you need to so it will fit in the pot. Do not remove the seeds yet. Once finished, use the quick release function to remove the pressure. Carefully take the lid off and allow to cool for about five minutes. Section into fourths, and check for doneness

2. If it is half done – cook again on high for 15 minutes.

3. If it is more than half done – cook again on high for 8 minutes.

4. If it is less than half done – cook again on high for 20 minutes.

5. How you plan on using the squash will dictated as to how done you need to make it. Once done, quick release the pressure and fix as you would like.

80 Crispy Potatoes

Prep Time: 5 minutes; **Cook Time**: 10 minutes

Recommended Serving Size: 1 cup; **Serves**: 3

Ingredients:

- ½ lemon
- ½ pound fingerling potatoes, peeled
- ¼ cup minced Italian parsley
- 1 tbsp. butter

Directions:

1. Put one half cup of water in the bottom of your pot. Place in the steamer insert.
2. Put the potatoes on the insert.
3. Cover with the lid and seal.
4. Cook on high for five minutes, and let the pressure release.
5. Take the potatoes out of the pot and discard water.
6. Set pot to sauté and melt the butter.
7. Place in the potatoes and season with pepper and salt.
8. Allow to sauté for a few minutes until crispy. Flip and brown the other side.
9. Squeeze on the lemon juice and toss with parsley.

81 Sweet Brussel Sprouts

Prep Time: 0 minutes; **Cook Time**: 4 minutes

Recommended Serving Size: 1 cup; **Serves**: 6

Ingredients:

- 2 tsp. orange zest
- 1 pound Brussel sprouts, trimmed
- 2 tbsp. butter
- 1 tbsp. maple syrup
- 6 tbsp. orange juice

Directions:

1. Put all of the ingredients in the pot, and seal the lid on.
2. Set on high for four minutes for tender sprouts. Cook for less if you prefer them crunchy.
3. Once finished, turn off, and quick release the pressure.
4. Give everything a stir to coat the sprouts.

82 Corn

Prep Time: 10 minutes; **Cook Time**: 22 minutes

Recommended Serving Size: 1 ear of corn; **Serves**: 2

Ingredients:

- 2 ears of corn
- 2 cups water

Directions:

1. Shuck and clean the corn. Add the water to the pot, and stack the corn inside vertically.

2. Close and seal the lid. Set on high for 2 minutes.

3. Allow the pressure to release naturally. This will take about 20 minutes.

83 Maple Bacon Squash

Prep Time: 0 minutes; **Cook Time**: 30 minutes

Recommended Serving Size: 1 cup; **Serves**: 6

Ingredients:

- Salt
- 2 tbsp. maple syrup
- 2 tbsp. butter
- ½ cup diced, cooked bacon
- 4 pounds acorn squash

Directions:

1. Put one cup of water into the instant pot, and set the trivet in. Place the squash on the trivet.
2. Close and seal the lid. Set to high for eight minutes. Once done, quick release pressure and allow to cool.
3. Carefully take out the squash. Slice them open and remove the seeds.
4. Add the squash back to the pot. Close and seal on the lid. Set to cook on high for eight minutes. Quick release the pressure and let it cool.
5. Remove the squash, and remove the flesh. Mash in the butter and syrup using a potato masher.
6. Mix in the bacon and salt, and mix well.

84 Buffalo Cauliflower

Prep Time: 5 minutes; **Cook Time**: 2 hours, 30 minutes

Recommended Serving Size: 1 cup; **Serves**: 6 to 8

Ingredients:

- ½ cup buffalo sauce
- 2 packages frozen cauliflower
- 1 cup shredded cheese
- 2 cans cheddar cheese soup

Directions:

1. Coat your instant pot with some nonstick spray.
2. Lightly thaw the cauliflower. Pour into a bowl, and stir in the rest of the ingredients. Season with pepper and salt.
3. Pour the mixture into the instant pot.
4. Close and seal the lid.
5. Set to slow cook on high for 2 and a half to three hours, or until tender.
6. Once done, quick release the pressure and enjoy.

85 Cheesy Broccoli

Prep Time: 5 minutes; **Cook Time**: 2 hours, 30 minutes

Recommended Serving Size: 1 cup; **Serves**: 6 to 8

Ingredients:

- Salt
- Pepper
- 2 packages frozen broccoli florets
- 1 cup shredded cheese
- 2 cans cheddar cheese soup

Directions:

1. Thaw the broccoli on the counter for one hour prior to cooking.
2. Put all of the ingredients in a bowl and mix to combine.
3. Pour the mixture into your instant pot. Close and seal the lid.
4. Set to slow cook on high for two and a half to three hours.
5. Once done, quick release the pressure and enjoy.

86 Cheesy Cauliflower

Prep Time: 5 minutes; **Cook Time**: 2 hours, 30 minutes

Recommended Serving Size: 1 cup; **Serves**: 6 to 8

Ingredients:

- 1 cup shredded cheese
- 2 packages frozen cauliflower
- Pepper
- Salt
- 2 cans cheddar cheese soup

Directions:

1. Thaw the cauliflower on the counter for one hour.
2. Put the cauliflower and the remaining ingredients in bowl and mix to combine.
3. Pour the mixture into your instant pot. Close and seal the lid.
4. Set to slow cook on high for two and a half hours to three hours.
5. Once done, quick release the pressure and enjoy.

87 Greek Fries

Prep Time: 5 minutes; **Cook Time**: 10 to 20 minutes

Recommended Serving Size: ¼ of the fries; **Serves**: 4

Ingredients:

- Oregano
- 4 large potatoes, cut into wedges
- 1 lemon
- 1/2 cup Feta cheese

Directions:

1. Set the trivet in the bottom of the pot and place the potatoes on top. Put in one cup of water.
2. Close and seal the lid. Set on high for two minutes.
3. Remove the potatoes carefully and dry them completely.
4. Empty out the water, and dry the instant pot.
5. Set to sauté and heat up some oil. Make sure it's hot before adding in the fries.
6. Add a few fries and cook until crisp. Continue until all fries are done.
7. Drain fries on paper towels.
8. Place on plate and squeeze on lemon juice. Sprinkle with Feta and oregano.
9. Enjoy.

88 Caramelized Onions

Prep Time: 10 minutes; **Cook Time**: 7 hours

Recommended Serving Size: ½ cup; **Serves**: 4

Ingredients:

- ¼ cup olive oil
- 3 large sliced sweet onions

Directions:

1. Put the olive oil in the instant pot.
2. Add the onions and toss to coat.
3. Close and seal the lid.
4. Set to slow cook on low for 7 hours.
5. Once done, quick release the pressure and use them as you would like.

89 Italian Potatoes

Prep Time: 5 minutes; **Cook Time**: 3 hours

Recommended Serving Size: 1 cup; **Serves**: 4

Ingredients:

- 1 packet Italian dressing mix
- 1 tbsp. olive oil
- 3 large yellow potatoes

Directions:

1. Clean the potatoes and cut into cubes.
2. Place them inside the instant pot.
3. Drizzle potatoes with oil and seasoning on both sides.
4. Close the lid and seal.
5. Set to slow cook on high for three hours.
6. Once done, quick release the pressure. Stir the potatoes gently. Enjoy.

90 Garlic Ranch Potatoes

Prep Time: 5 minutes; **Cook Time**: 4 hours

Recommended Serving Size: 1 cup; **Serves**: 6 to 8

Ingredients:

- 3 pounds red potatoes, quartered
- 2 tbsp. olive oil
- 2 tbsp. salted butter
- 1 packet ranch dressing mix
- 1 tbsp. minced garlic

Directions:

1. Spray the instant pot with cooking spray.
2. Put all of the ingredients in the pot. Mix in some pepper and salt and stir together.
3. Close the lid and seal.
4. Set to slow cook on high for four hours until fork tender.
5. Once done, quick release the pressure.
6. Serve hot.

91 Roast Vegetables

Prep Time: 10 minutes; **Cook Time**: 3 hours

Recommended Serving Size: ½ cup; **Serves**: 4

Ingredients:

- 1 large sweet potato, cubed and peeled
- ½ cup peeled garlic cloves
- 2 bell peppers, cut into large slices, ribs and seeds removed
- 3 small zucchini, thickly sliced
- Herbs and spice of choice

Directions:

1. Spray the instant pot with cooking spray.
2. Place all the veggies into the pot.
3. Drizzle with a little oil and add in herbs and spices. Stir to coat.
4. Close the lid and seal.
5. Set to slow cook on high for three hours.
6. Use quick release the pressure.
7. Remove the veggies and enjoy.

Desserts

92 Baked Apples

Prep Time: 10 minutes; **Cook Time**: 40 minutes

Recommended Serving Size: 1 apple; **Serves**: 4

Ingredients:

- 1 tsp. cinnamon
- 4 apples, cored
- ½ cup sugar
- 6 tbsp. raisins
- ½ cup red wine

Directions:

1. Wash and dry the apples. Put the apples in the instant pot. Add the cinnamon, sugar, raisins, and wine.

2. Lock the lid on. Set on high for ten minutes. Once done, allow the pressure to release naturally.

3. Carefully take the apples out and serve with any remaining liquid.

93 Chocolate Fondue

Prep Time: 0 minutes; **Cook Time**: 10 minutes

Recommended Serving Size: 3.5 oz.; **Serves**: 2

Ingredients:

- 3.5 ounces fresh cream
- 3.5 ounces bittersweet chocolate

Directions:

1. Put two cups of water and the trivet in the instant pot.
2. Put the ingredients into a heatproof bowl. Set the bowl inside the instant pot.
3. Set on high for two minutes. Release the pressure slowly.
4. Carefully remove the bowl. Stir until the chocolate comes together.
5. Serve with fruits and bread of choice.

94 Crème Brulee

Prep Time: 0 minutes; **Cook Time**: 2 hours, 6 minutes

Recommended Serving Size: 1 cup; **Serves**: 4

Ingredients:

- 8 egg yolks
- 1 ½ tsp. vanilla
- 6 tbsp. sugar
- 6 tbsp. superfine sugar
- 2 cups heavy cream

Directions:

1. Put a cup and a half of water into the instant pot. Add the trivet.

2. Mix the yolks and sugar together. Add a pinch of salt. Add the vanilla and cream. Mix well. Strain into a pitcher, and pour into four custard cups. Place the foil on top of each cup. Place the cups on the trivet.

3. Seal the lid. Set on high for six minutes. Release the pressure carefully. Uncover and allow to cool.

4. Place the plastic wrap on top and put in the refrigerator for two hours.

5. When ready to eat, sprinkle tops with superfine sugar. Use a blow torch to brown the sugar.

95 Dulce De Leche

Prep Time: 0 minutes; **Cook Time**: 1 hour

Recommended Serving Size: ¼ cup; **Serves**: Varies

Ingredients:

- 1 can sweetened condensed milk

Directions:

1. Place the can on its side on the bottom of the instant pot. Add cold water until it reaches an inch above the can. Seal the lid into place.

2. Set the pot to cook on high for 40 minutes. Turn off and let all of the pressure to release naturally

3. Carefully take the can out of the pot. Open the can and use as you would like.

96 Red Wine Pears

Prep Time: 5 minutes; **Cook Time**: 25 minutes

Recommended Serving Size: 1 pear; **Serves**: 2

Ingredients:

- 2 pears, peeled
- 1 whole clove
- ½ bottle favorite red wine
- ½ cup sugar
- Piece of ginger

Directions:

1. Put the wine into the instant pot. Add the clove, sugar, and ginger. Place the pears into the pot, and lock on lid.

2. Set on high for six minutes. Once done, allow all of the pressure to release naturally. Carefully take the pears out.

3. Turn the pot to sauté. Heat to boil and let the liquid reduce. Drizzle the liquid over the pears and sprinkle with some cinnamon.

97 Pots de Creme

Prep Time: 0 minutes; **Cook Time**: 1 hour

Recommended Serving Size: ½ cup; **Serves**: 4

Ingredients:

- 1 cup fresh cream
- 1 lemon
- 1 cup whole milk
- ¾ cup white sugar
- 6 egg yolks

Directions:

1. Zest the lemon. Add the zest, milk, and cream to a saucepan. Let everything come to a bubble. Remove from the heat and completely cool.

2. Whisk the yolks and sugar together. Pour in the cream mixture slowly. Try not to overmix. Pour through a strainer.

3. Pour the smooth mixture into ramekins. Pour in the barest amount of water into your instant pot. Add the trivet. Cover the ramekins with foil and place them in the pot. Lock and seal the lid.

4. Set on high for ten minutes. Let the pressure release naturally.

5. Take out the ramekins from the instant pot carefully. Allow them to sit for 40 minutes. Serve with blackberries if desired.

98 Egg Custard

Prep Time: 5 minutes; **Cook Time**: 10 minutes

Recommended Serving Size: 1 ramekin; **Serves**: 4

Ingredients:

- 1 ½ cups whole milk, divided
- 3 large eggs
- Pinch salt
- 4 to 5 tbsp. sugar

Directions:

1. Put the milk, salt, and sugar in the instant pot. Set to the slow cook function on low. Stir until the sugar melts.

2. Turn off and allow the milk to cool a bit.

3. Add a half cup of whole milk to the milk mixture and mix well. This should be cool to the touch.

4. Crack all of the eggs into a bowl, and beat them together. Pour the milk mixture in the eggs while you are whisking. Make sure to mix well.

5. Pour the mixture through a strainer twice to get rid of any solids, this makes the mixture silky smooth

6. Pour the mixture into 4 ramekins. Tap gently to get rid of any air bubbles. Cover with foil.

7. Pour one cup of water in the pot. Put in the trivet. Place the ramekins on the trivet.

8. Close and seal the lid.

9. Set to slow cook on low for zero minutes. This is not a typo. Then use the natural pressure release for ten minutes.

10. Carefully remove. Serve warm.

99 Key Lime Dump Cake

Prep Time: 5 minutes; **Cook Time**: 2 hours

Recommended Serving Size: 1 cup; **Serves**: 8

Ingredients:

- 2 cans key lime pie filling
- ½ c butter, melted
- 1 French vanilla, box mix

Directions:

1. Coat the inside of your instant pot with cooking spray.
2. Put the cans of pie filling in the bottom and spread evenly.
3. Mix together the butter and cake mix. Stir until crumbly.
4. Put the cake batter over the pie filling.
5. Set on slow cook on high for two hours.
6. Once done, quick release the pressure.
7. Serve with ice cream or whipped cream.

100 Monkey Bread

Prep Time: 10 minutes; **Cook Time**: 2 hours, 30 minutes
Recommended Serving Size: 1 cup; **Serves**: 6 to 8

Ingredients:

- ½ cup brown sugar, packed
- 1 can large biscuits
- 1 tsp. ground cinnamon
- 1 stick butter, melted
- ½ cup granulated sugar

Directions:

1. Spray the instant pot with cooking spray.
2. Melt the butter in a microwave safe bowl.
3. Place the cinnamon and sugars in a gallon storage bag. Close and shake to mix well.
4. Cut the individual biscuits into six pieces. Dip each piece into melted butter, and place in the bag with cinnamon sugar.
5. When all pieces are in the bag, shake well to coat.
6. Put the remaining butter in the bottom of the instant pot.
7. Put all the coated biscuits into the instant pot in an even layer.
8. Set to slow cook on high for two and a half hours.

9. Once done, quick release the pressure.

10. You can make some icing with powdered sugar and milk to serve on top.

11. Scoop into bowls and enjoy.

101 Hot Fudge Cake

Prep Time: 5 minutes; **Cook Time**: 1 hour, 30 minutes
Recommended Serving Size: 1 cup; **Serves**: 8

Ingredients:

- ¾ c vegetable oil
- 4 eggs
- 1 box chocolate fudge cake mix
- 2/3 c sour cream
- 1 chocolate pudding, instant

Directions:

1. Mix the oil, sour cream, eggs, pudding mix, and cake mix together using an electric mixer until smooth
2. Spray the instant pot with cooking spray. Pour the mixture in the pot.
3. Set to slow cook on high for one and a half hours.
4. Once done, use the quick release to remove the pressure.
5. Take the lid off carefully and spoon out into bowls.
6. Drizzle with hot fudge sauce and serve hot with ice cream.

102 Chocolate Cherry Cake

Prep Time: 5 minutes; **Cook Time**: 2 hours

Recommended Serving Size: 1 cup; **Serves**: 8

Ingredients:

- 2 cans cherry pie filling
- ½ c butter, melted
- 1 devil's food cake, box mix

Directions:

1. Spray the instant pot with nonstick spray.
2. Place the cherry filling in the bottom and spread evenly.
3. Combine the cake mix and butter, mix until crumbly.
4. Put in an even layer on top of the pie filling.
5. Set the pot to slow cook, and set for two hours on high.
6. Once done, quick release the pressure.
7. Serve with ice cream or whipped cream.

103 Caramel Apple Cake

Prep Time: 5 minutes; **Cook Time**: 2 hours

Recommended Serving Size: 1 cup; **Serves**: 8

Ingredients:

- 1 yellow cake, box mix
- ½ c butter, melted
- 2 cans apple pie filling
- ½ cup caramel syrup

Directions:

1. Spray your pot with some nonstick spray
2. Put the pie filling in the bottom and spread evenly.
3. Mix the cake mix and melted butter until crumbly.
4. Place in an even layer on top of the pie filling.
5. Close and seal the lid.
6. Set to slow cook on high for two hours.
7. Once done, quick release the pressure.
8. Serve with ice cream or whipped cream.

104 Pumpkin Spice Cake

Prep Time: 5 minutes; **Cook Time**: 1 hour, 30 minutes

Recommended Serving Size: 1 cup; **Serves**: 8

Ingredients:

- 1 tsp. pumpkin pie spice
- 1 can pumpkin puree
- ½ c applesauce
- 3 eggs
- 1 spice cake, box mix

Directions:

1. Coat the inside of your instant pot with nonstick spray.
2. Mix all the ingredients together with a hand mixer for one minute.
3. Pour the mixture into your instant pot.
4. Close and seal the lid.
5. Set to slow cook on high for one and a half hours.
6. Once done, use the quick pressure function to remove the pressure.
7. Scoop the cake into bowls and top with cream cheese frosting.

105 Lemon Blueberry Cake

Prep Time: 5 minutes; **Cook Time**: 2 hours

Recommended Serving Size: 1 cup; **Serves**: 8

Ingredients:

- 2 cans blueberry pie filling
- 1 stick melted butter
- 1 lemon cake, box mix

Directions:

1. Spray the instant pot with cooking spray.
2. Put the pie filling in your instant pot and spread it around.
3. Mix the cake mix and melted butter until crumbly.
4. Close and seal the lid.
5. Set your instant pot to slow cook for two hours on high.
6. Once done, quick release the pressure
7. Serve with ice cream or whipped cream.

106 Strawberry Cake

Prep Time: 5 minutes; **Cook Time**: 2 hours

Recommended Serving Size: 1 cup; **Serves**: 8

Ingredients:

- 2 cans strawberry pie filling
- ½ c butter, melted
- 1 strawberry cake, box mix

Directions:

1. Spray the instant pot with cooking spray.
2. Put the pie filling in the bottom and spread evenly.
3. Mix the cake mix and butter together until crumbly.
4. Close and seal the lid.
5. Set you pot to slow cook for two hours on high.
6. Once done, quick release the pressure.
7. Serve with ice cream or whipped cream.

107 Red Velvet Cake

Prep Time: 5 minutes; **Cook Time**: 1 hour, 30 minutes

Recommended Serving Size: 1 cup; **Serves**: 8

Ingredients:

- 1 1/3 c water
- 1 red velvet, box mix
- ½ c applesauce
- 3 eggs

Directions:

1. Coat your pot with nonstick spray.
2. Mix all of the ingredients together using a hand mixer for one minute.
3. Pour into the instant pot, and seal on the lid.
4. Set to slow cook on high for one and a half hours.
5. Once done, quick release the pressure.
6. Serve with cream cheese frosting or ice cream.

108 Peach Cobbler

Prep Time: 15 minutes; **Cook Time**: 20 minutes

Recommended Serving Size: 1 cup; **Serves**: 6

Ingredients:

- 6 to 8 peaches, peeled and sliced
- ¼ cup softened butter
- 1 box white cake mix, halved

Directions:

1. Mix ½ of the cake mix and butter in a bowl until crumbly. Use a pastry cutter if it will make it easier.

2. Put the peaches into heat proof bowl, and sprinkle with the cake mix.

3. Cover with foil. Set the trivet into your instant pot. Add in a cup of water. Lower the bowl onto the trivet.

4. Close the lid and seal.

5. Set to manual for ten minutes.

6. Once done, naturally release the pressure for about ten minutes. Then quick release the rest of the pressure.

7. Remove the lid, and take the cobbler out carefully.

8. Serve with ice cream or whipped cream.

109 Lemon Cake

Prep Time: 5 minutes; **Cook Time**: 2 hours

Recommended Serving Size: 1 cup; **Serves**: 8

Ingredients:

- 1 stick melted butter
- 2 21 oz cans lemon crème pie filling
- 1 box lemon cake mix

Directions:

1. Spray inside of the instant pot with cooking spray.
2. Empty out the cans of pie filling in the bottom of the instant pot. Spread into an even layer.
3. In a mixing bowl, mix the dry cake mix with the melted butter. Stir until it becomes crumbly. If there are any large chunks, break them up with the spoon.
4. Pour the crumble over the pie filling and spread into an even layer.
5. Close and seal lid.
6. Set to slow cook on high and cook for two hours.
7. When finished, quick release pressure. Scoop out and serve with either ice cream or whipped topping.

Conclusion

Thank you again for buying and reading, *"Instant Pot Cookbook: 5 Ingredients or Less – Quick, Easy and Healthy Meals for Your Family."*

Creating delicious and nutritious meals doesn't have to be a pain. You can simply pop a few ingredients into your **Instant Pot**, press a few buttons, and leave the kitchen for much needed rest and relaxation. When you come back, a warm dish is waiting for you.

Hopefully, by trying out some of the recipes in this book, you will be encouraged to create your own, so that you can share your tasty dishes to family and friends.

Finally, if you enjoyed this book, then I'd like to ask you for a favor, would you be kind enough to leave a review for this book on Amazon? It'd be greatly appreciated!

Thank you and good luck on your cooking journey!

65734933R00080

Made in the USA
San Bernardino, CA
04 January 2018